The Official
Celtic Football Club
Annual 2012

Written by Joe Sullivan & Mark Henderson

ᵍ

A Grange Publication

© 2011. Published by Grange Communications Ltd., Edinburgh,
under licence from Celtic Football Club. Printed in the EU.

Photographs © Alan Whyte, Angus Johnston,
SNS Group, Shutterstock.com

ISBN 978 1 908221 20 9

CONTENTS

CLUB HONOURS

Scottish League Winners [42 times]

1892/93, 1893/94, 1895/96, 1897/98,
1904/05, 1905/06, 1906/07, 1907/08,
1908/09, 1909/10, 1913/14, 1914/15,
1915/16, 1916/17, 1918/19, 1921/22,
1925/26, 1935/36, 1937/38, 1953/54,
1965/66, 1966/67, 1967/68, 1968/69,
1969/70, 1970/71, 1971/72, 1972/73,
1973/74, 1976/77, 1978/79, 1980/81,
1981/82, 1985/86, 1987/88, 1997/98,
2000/01, 2001/02, 2003/04, 2005/06,
2006/07, 2007/08

Scottish Cup Winners [35 times]

1892, 1899, 1900, 1904, 1907, 1908,
1911, 1912, 1914, 1923, 1925, 1927,
1931, 1933, 1937, 1951, 1954, 1965,
1967, 1969, 1971, 1972, 1974, 1975,
1977, 1980, 1985, 1988, 1989, 1995,
2001, 2004, 2005, 2007, 2011

League Cup Winners [14 times]

1956/57, 1957/58, 1965/66, 1966/67,
1967/68, 1968/69, 1969/70, 1974/75,
1982/83, 1997/98, 1999/00, 2000/01,
2005/06, 2008/09

European Cup Winners 1967

Coronation Cup Winners 1953

MANAGER FACTFILE

NEIL LENNON

D.O.B: 25/06/71

Born: Lurgan, Nothern Ireland

Playing career record:

Manchester City (1989-90), Crewe Alexandra
(1990-96), Leicester City (1996-2000),
Celtic (2000-07), Nottingham Forest (2007-08),
Wycombe Wanderers (2008).

Playing honours:

Leicester City - League Cup Winners:
1996/97, 1999/00

Celtic - Scottish Premier League Champions:
2000/01, 2001/02, 2003/04, 2005/06, 2006/07

Scottish Cup Winners:
2001, 2004, 2005, 2007

Scottish League Cup Winners:
2000/01, 2005/06

UEFA Cup Runners-up:
2002/03

As Manager - Celtic - Scottish Cup:
2010/11

NEIL LENNON initially took up the reins at Celtic when the team was floundering in choppy waters near the end of the 2009/10 season and he steered the side back on an even keel.

It was at the end of March 2010 that the Irishman took charge as interim manager and he quickly settled the team as the Hoops won their eight remaining matches in the SPL.

The only downside was defeat in the semi-final of the Scottish Cup but after being confirmed as the new manager on June 9, 2010, Lennon went on to repay the faith shown in him by the Celtic board by delivering that very trophy less than a year later as the new-look Hoops finished the manager's first full season on a high.

At the same Hampden venue a few months earlier, the Celts just missed out on the Co-operative Insurance Cup by virtue of an extra-time goal and, a week prior to the Scottish Cup victory, Lennon's side narrowly lost their fight for the championship by just one point. However, amid incredible scenes at Celtic Park, the green and white masses displayed complete solidarity

with a massive impromptu Huddle and backed the manager to the hilt after a stressful season for him off the park.

Just seconds after the final whistle, the manager took the microphone at a still packed Celtic Park and proclaimed: "This is not the end – this is just the beginning."

The following weekend his words proved true as his Celtic side, a team he and his backroom team of Johan Mjallby, Alan Thompson and Garry Parker, crafted from the remnants of the old side, went out and lifted the silverware at the showpiece game of the season.

The manager had been proved right in pinpointing key players to come in and re-affirm his pledge to bring the thunder back to Celtic Park.

He has certainly conveyed his winning mentality as a player in the green and white to equal success as Celtic manager with the team producing many performances throughout the season worthy of many of the great Celtic teams of the past – including the one he played in under Martin O'Neill.

Indeed, the last time Celtic lifted the Scottish Cup was in 2007 when it was Neil Lennon who raised the trophy aloft as captain of the Hoops.

The players wanted him to lift the trophy once more but he insisted that Scott Brown have his moment in raising his first silverware as skipper, but no-one was cheered as loudly that day at Hampden as Neil Lennon when he displayed the Scottish Cup to the Celtic support from the pitch.

For that Celtic support knew that if Neil Lennon hadn't been out on that pitch with the cup as manager of the club, he would have been in among them cheering another trophy win for the Hoops.

SEASON REVIEW
JULY/AUGUST

HAVING been handed the manager's job on a permanent basis in June, Neil Lennon and his newly hand-picked backroom staff of Johan Mjallby, Alan Thompson and Garry Parker quickly set about strengthening the squad.

And the manager didn't hang about as former Celt Charlie Mulgrew and Korean internationalist Cha Du-Ri were signed before the new backroom Bhoys were announced and Wales midfielder Joe Ledley joined soon after as the Celts jetted off to the States on their pre-season tour.

They were soon joined by Irishman Daryl Murphy, Mexican Efrain Juarez, Israeli internationalist Beram Kayal and Englishman Gary Hooper before the end of the month but August would also be busy on the transfer front.

Sweden's Daniel Majstorovic was next to join and he was followed by Honduran internationalist, Emilio Izaguirre, while keeper Fraser Forster arrived on loan from Newcastle United and the final new Bhoy before the transfer window closed was Anthony Stokes.

FLASH BACK

25 August 1993

ARBROATH'S Gayfield Park was the venue when Danny McGrain's side awaited the visit of his former club in the League Cup with many of the home fans sporting masks of the former Celt.

There was no hiding place for his charges though as the Hoops raced to a 9-1 win with Mark McNally, Pat McGinlay and Charlie Nicholas all netting goals while Frank McAvennie and Andy Payton stole the limelight with a hat-trick each.

Amid all this transfer activity, the action had moved from friendlies to competitive action which got off to an unfortunate start in the Champions League qualifiers when the Hoops lost 4-2 on aggregate to eventual Europa League finalists, SC Braga.

There was a similar story in the Europa League with a 4-2 aggregate defeat to FC Utrecht but on the domestic front, the Hoops got off on the right foot with a 1-0 away victory over Inverness CT and a 4-0 home win over St Mirren before ending the month with a 1-0 victory over Motherwell.

BIRTHDAY BHOYS
James Forrest - July 7, 1991
Jimmy Quinn - July 8, 1878
Kris Commons - August 30, 1983
Bobby Murdoch - August 17, 1944

SEPTEMBER

THE new month started pretty quietly as international football tied up the action for the best part of two weeks but the Hoops soon got back into the swing of things with the visit of Hearts.

The Tynecastle side were put to the sword with a wee bit to spare as James Forrest and Shaun Maloney put Celtic 2-0 up before another trademark solo goal from Paddy McCourt tied the game up at 3-0.

Next up was a trip to Rugby Park and Kilmarnock put up more of a fight by taking the lead before an Irish strike-force pulled the game back in Celtic's favour as Daryl Murphy scored from the spot while Anthony Stokes joined him on the scoresheet by scoring his first goal for Celtic.

Inverness Caley Thistle then made the midweek trip down on Co-operative Insurance Cup duty but found themselves on the wrong side of a sparkling Celtic performance as the Hoops hit them for six.

BIRTHDAY BHOYS
Thomas Rogne - September 26, 1990
Jimmy Delaney - September 3, 1914

Top hit-man for the night was Georgios Samaras as the big Greek striker netted a hat-trick while Stokes scored twice and the other goal came from Gary Hooper in the 6-0 win.

The month ended with the visit of Hibernian and it was former Easter Road favourite Scott Brown who opened the scoring for Celtic while Glenn Loovens made it 2-0 after the break before Hibs pulled one back but the game finished 2-1 to the Hoops.

FLASH BACK

03
September 1966

IN the 65th minute of a 1-0 victory over St Mirren at Love Street in the League Cup, Jimmy Johnstone was helped off the park after suffering from mild concussion following a head knock.

Jock Stein moved Tommy Gemmell up to attack on the left wing and sent on Willie O'Neill to the left-back position – and so the defender became the first ever Celtic substitute as the rule had only been introduced that year.

OCTOBER

HAMILTON Accies were the first visitors of the new month but the Lanarkshire side also managed to score the first goal of October when they took a shock lead at Celtic Park.

The New Douglas Park outfit also managed to keep Fraser Forster busy but he pulled off a few great saves before Shaun Maloney restored parity when he netted the equaliser and the same scorer later put Celtic ahead while the job was finished by Gary Hooper who made it 3-1.

Next up was a trip to Tannadice with two Hooper goals, the second in the last minute, giving Celtic a 2-1 win. But it was the cancellation of a penalty awarded to the Hoops and the surrounding furore that made all the headlines.

There were more strange decisions the following week when Rangers won 3-1 at Celtic Park but the Hoops got back on the winning track in midweek with a visit to McDiarmid Park on Co-operative Insurance Cup duty.

Celtic sped to a three-goal lead in the first 13 minutes but St Johnstone fought back with two goals to make for a slightly nervy ending just days before the Hoops returned to Perth on league duty.

This time the visiting Celts scored three goals with no reply from the Saints as two Niall McGinn counters sandwiched a spectacular conversion from Emilio Izaguirre with the Honduran defender netting his first goal for the team.

FLASH BACK

19
October
1957

CELTIC went into the 1957 League Cup final as holders but not favourites with Rangers expected to leave Hampden with the trophy but the Ibrox side ended up leaving with their tails between their legs.

This historic day gave birth to the legend "Oh Hampden in the Sun, Celtic seven Rangers one" as the Hoops went on the rampage and despite the ball coming back off the woodwork on numerous occasions, they still managed to win 7-1.

BIRTHDAY BHOYS
Glenn Loovens - October 22, 1983
Jimmy Kelly - October 15, 1865

NOVEMBER

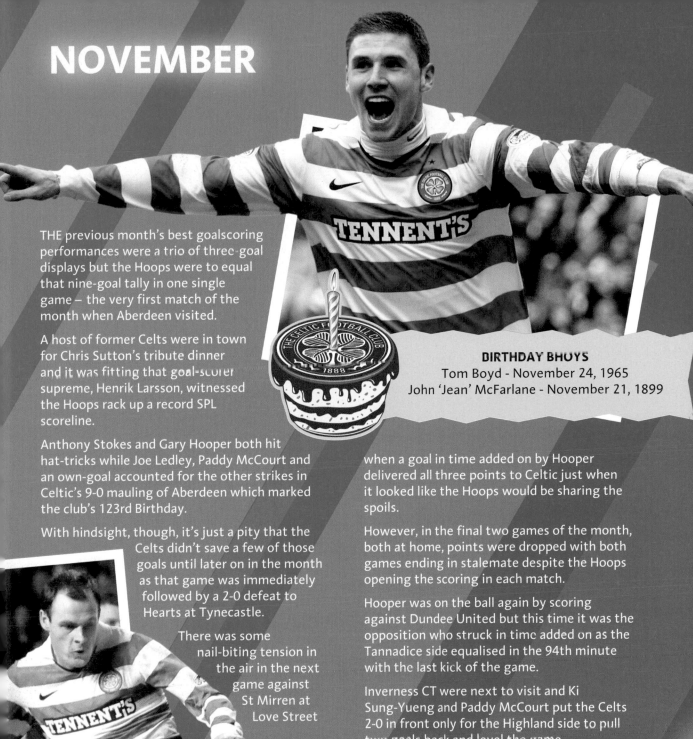

THE previous month's best goalscoring performances were a trio of three-goal displays but the Hoops were to equal that nine-goal tally in one single game – the very first match of the month when Aberdeen visited.

A host of former Celts were in town for Chris Sutton's tribute dinner and it was fitting that goal-scorer supreme, Henrik Larsson, witnessed the Hoops rack up a record SPL scoreline.

Anthony Stokes and Gary Hooper both hit hat-tricks while Joe Ledley, Paddy McCourt and an own-goal accounted for the other strikes in Celtic's 9-0 mauling of Aberdeen which marked the club's 123rd Birthday.

With hindsight, though, it's just a pity that the Celts didn't save a few of those goals until later on in the month as that game was immediately followed by a 2-0 defeat to Hearts at Tynecastle.

There was some nail-biting tension in the air in the next game against St Mirren at Love Street

BIRTHDAY BHOYS
Tom Boyd - November 24, 1965
John 'Jean' McFarlane - November 21, 1899

when a goal in time added on by Hooper delivered all three points to Celtic just when it looked like the Hoops would be sharing the spoils.

However, in the final two games of the month, both at home, points were dropped with both games ending in stalemate despite the Hoops opening the scoring in each match.

Hooper was on the ball again by scoring against Dundee United but this time it was the opposition who struck in time added on as the Tannadice side equalised in the 94th minute with the last kick of the game.

Inverness CT were next to visit and Ki Sung-Yueng and Paddy McCourt put the Celts 2-0 in front only for the Highland side to pull two goals back and level the game.

FLASH BACK

06 November 1887

THIS was the day that it all started, for it was on this day in 1887 that a group of men met in St Mary's Parish Hall to discuss Brother Walfrid's vision of starting a football team to help feed the poor in the East End of Glasgow.

Local businessman John Glass chaired the meeting and the new club was formally constituted with the votes cast in favour of Brother Walfrid's suggestion of the name – Celtic Football Club.

11

DECEMBER

THE worst winter weather in living memory played havoc with the football schedule and the Hoops had the opening three games of the month – Aberdeen away, Kilmarnock at home and Hamilton Accies away – postponed amid the freezing conditions.

However, some football did break out among the snowball fights of Scotland but the Hoops had to settle for their third successive home draw when the Kilmarnock game was re-scheduled and this time it was Celtic who had to come from behind when Thomas Rogne equalised in the 84th minute.

That game was played on the 21st of the month and Celtic managed to play their other two scheduled games starting with the Boxing Day visit of St Johnstone and had the South Korean duo of Ki Sung-Yueng and Cha Du-Ri to thank for the 2-0 win…

And it was another late, late show with both scorers finding the net in the 90th minute to wrap up a nice Christmas present for the Celtic crowd with Cha netting first before being quickly followed by Ki with the last kick of the ball.

That left the final game of 2010 as Motherwell made the short trip up from Lanarkshire on Hogmanay and it was Paddy McCourt who ensured the Celtic fans would be celebrating that night when he scored the only goal of the game in the 27th minute.

However, a soft second yellow for Scott Brown ensured that the skipper would miss the first game of 2011 when the Hoops would travel to Ibrox to play Rangers.

25 December 1965

FLASH BACK

CELTIC have recorded a few decent scores on Christmas Day, starting with a 9-1 win over Clyde in 1897 and they also beat Airdrie 6-0 in 1915 and hammered Kilmarnock 8-0 in 1937.

Another high-scoring Christmas present arrived in 1965 when Morton were sent home on the back of an 8-1 defeat with Joe McBride scoring a hat-trick as the Celts sped to a 7-0 half-time lead before John Hughes wrapped up the day with the eighth in the 80th minute. .

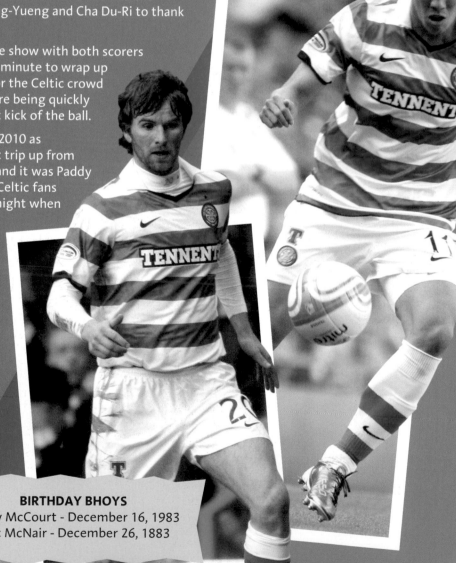

BIRTHDAY BHOYS
Paddy McCourt - December 16, 1983
Alec McNair - December 26, 1883

JANUARY

THE Hoops managed to squeeze seven games into the first month of the year and 2011 couldn't have got off to a better start thanks to a magnificent 2-0 win at Ibrox with Greek striker Georgios Samaras scoring twice.

With that opening win under the belt, the Hoops took on Rangers again the following week – Berwick Rangers that is – and the Scottish Cup tie gave Neil Lennon the opportunity to ease in former Arsenal favourite, Freddie Ljungberg, who had signed on from Chicago Fire.

However, it was Daniel Majstorovic, with his first goal for the club, and skipper Scott Brown who stole the limelight by finding the net in the 2-0 victory in Celtic's opening Scottish Cup outing of the season.

Next up was Hamilton Accies in the re-arranged game and literally nothing went right for Celtic on the night as a 1-1 draw was salvaged from potential defeat by the 10-man Celts, but the next game's scoreline was far more comprehensive.

Easter Road was the venue and Gary Hooper opened the scoring in the first half before an Anthony Stokes penalty was followed up by a spectacular overhead free-kick by the Irish striker to make the final score 3-0.

Aberdeen arrived the following weekend and there was no repeat of the previous outright thrashing but the Hoops still took all three points thanks to Stokes finding the net again.

The same striker struck twice in the next game and he was joined on the scoresheet by James Forrest and Paddy McCourt as Celtic beat Hearts 4-0, but in the next game there was a new name among the scorers.

Kris Commons arrived from Derby County and the new Celt took just six minutes to open his account as the Hoops beat Aberdeen 4-1 in the Co-operative Insurance Cup semi-final at Hampden.

FLASH BACK

14 January 1928

CELTIC'S all-time top goal-scorer, Jimmy McGrory, had scored two successive singles followed by two consecutive hat-tricks prior to the Hoops welcoming Dunfermline Athletic on league duty.

However, although he may have been on a high after scoring eight goals in four games, nothing prepared him for what happened next as he managed to find the net EIGHT times in Celtic's 9-0 win over the Fife side.

BIRTHDAY BHOYS
Gary Hooper - January 26, 1988
'Sunny' Jim Young - January 10, 1882

FEBRUARY

FRESH from beating Aberdeen 4-1 in the League Cup semi-final, the Celts took on the Pittodrie side again in the league just three days later and there was no surprise when the strike duo of Gary Hooper and Anthony Stokes got on the scoresheet.

However, in his 102nd game for the Hoops, Mark Wilson finally got off the mark with his first goal – and that 3-0 win wouldn't be the last game in which he would find the net.

Rangers at Ibrox were next in the Scottish Cup and despite going down to 10 men when keeper Fraser Forster was sent off at the expense of a penalty, the Celts came from behind and Kris Commons' goal was topped by a scorcher from Scott Brown with the Hoops claiming all the plaudits in the 2-2 draw.

Next up was Celtic's fourth consecutive game away from home and Wilson found the net again – this time in a 3-1 win over his former club, Dundee United, at Tannadice as the Hoops readied themselves for another league visit from Rangers.

Hooper struck twice in the first half as the Hoops carved Rangers open and another Commons' spectacular in the second half finished off the 3-0 scoreline for the Hoops and the first mass Huddle by the supporters went ahead at Celtic Park.

The month ended on a low point, though, when a trip to Fir Park saw a 2-0 defeat as the Celts missed Beram Kayal who had been a stand-out performer over the previous two months since his return from injury.

29
February 1960

FLASH BACK

FOLLOWING successive 1-1 and 4-4 Scottish Cup draws against St Mirren, the Hoops finally leapt forward in one of the few Leap Year February 29ths in which they have been in action.

At the third attempt, Celtic saw off the Paisley side with Neilly Mochan, who had already scored twice in the 4-4 game, netting all FIVE goals in the Hoops' 5-2 win.

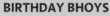

BIRTHDAY BHOYS
Filip and Patrik Twardzik - February 10, 1993
Bobby Collins - February 16, 1931

MARCH

FIRST up was the visit of Rangers in the Scottish Cup replay and not content with scoring twice the previous month, Mark Wilson notched the only goal of the game as the Hoops came out on top in a night of drama at Celtic Park.

The defender hit his third goal in four weeks when his initial shot was blocked on the line and his return volley dug into the turf before rising into the back of the net and sending Celtic Park into raptures.

Following the Wednesday night excitement, Hamilton Accies visited on the Saturday and two goals from Kris Commons sealed the points for Celtic in a 2-0 win in the Hoops' only league meeting of the month.

The Scottish Cup was on the agenda next and the win over Rangers was rewarded with a difficult trip north to play Inverness Caley Thistle in the quarter-final and the home side took the lead from the penalty spot just a minute before half-time.

However, Joe Ledley levelled almost immediately and the Welshman struck again in the second half and Celtic went through to the semi-final courtesy of the 2-1 win in the Highlands.

There was more cup action four days later, this time in the League Cup final when the Celts met Rangers at Hampden in the last game of the month.

There was, however, to be no silverware joy for Celtic on this occasion as, despite Joe Ledley leveling the game at 1-1 in the first half, it was the Ibrox side who broke the deadlock in extra-time for a 2-1 win.

FLASH BACK

21
March 1925

SUCH was the fervour surrounding the Scottish Cup semi-final between Celtic and Rangers, the game was switched to Hampden and the first six-figure crowd in Scotland, 101,714, attended the match.

The Hoops won 5-0 and went on to the final where Dundee were defeated 2-1 in what became known as The Patsy Gallacher final thanks to the Irishman's solo goal.

BIRTHDAY BHOYS
Charlie Mulgrew – March 6, 1986
Billy McNeill – March 2, 1940

APRIL

05

April 1969

AFTER winning three League Cup finals on the trot, Celtic went into yet another when they met Hibernian at Hampden and the Hoops came up trumps with the first part of that season's Treble.

Top man on the day was Bobby Lennox who hit a hat-trick in the 6-2 win over the Edinburgh side and the Hoops would also win the next League Cup to make it five-in-a-row.

CELTIC kicked-off the new month by welcoming Hibernian to the East End of Glasgow and looked to be on easy street by marking up a 3-0 score by half-time thanks to a goal by Anthony Stokes and a double from Gary Hooper, one of them from the spot.

The Easter Road side managed to pull one back, also from the spot, but former Celt Liam Miller's strike proved to be the only goal that Celtic would concede during the month of April.

St Mirren visited just three days later and this time it was substitute Kris Commons who struck with the only goal of the game in the 78th minute soon after replacing Freddie Ljungberg.

There was another single-goal win in the next game as the Hoops travelled to Perth to take on St Johnstone and the Celts in the McDiarmid Park crowd were in raptures when Beram Kayal scored his first goal for the club to claim the three points.

The next two wins were achieved rather more comprehensively as trips to Hampden and Kilmarnock yielded 4-0 wins for the Bhoys with Aberdeen providing the opposition at the National Stadium in the semi-final of the Scottish Cup.

It was more or less a repeat of the Co-operative Insurance Cup semi-final against the Dons with Charlie Mulgrew, Joe Ledley, Kris Commons and Shaun Maloney netting in the 4-0 win.

Kilmarnock fell by the same scoreline three days later in the league at Rugby Park with Commons netting twice while Stokes and Hooper also got on the scoresheet ahead of a trip to Ibrox for the seventh and final derby meeting of the season.

Once more the Hoops kept a clean sheet but also failed to score at the other end and the 0-0 draw in a six-pointer would prove decisive at the end of the term.

BIRTHDAY BHOYS
Daniel Majstorovic - April 5, 1977
Neilly Mochan - April 6, 1927

MAY

IT WAS a month in which injuries were to prove costly as key players Joe Ledley and Beram Kayal were both to drop out although the Israeli was to play two games before being counted out.

Indeed, he scored in the first game of the month when Kris Commons, Gary Hooper and Daryl Murphy joined him on the scoresheet in a 4-1 win over Dundee United at Celtic Park.

It was in the event, however, of trying to carve open another chance in the next game at Inverness, that the midfielder sustained the injury that kept him out for the rest of the season – but even bleaker was the fact that Celtic lost the game 3-2.

After that, in a sense, the injuries meant little as the Hoops secured full points from their three remaining games while the hoped-for slip from Rangers never materialised and the possibility of the league title slipped from Celtic's hands.

Kilmarnock were defeated 2-0 at Rugby Park while the potentially difficult trip to Tynecastle to take on Hearts was overcome with some ease in a 3-0 win for the Hoops just a few days prior to the last game of the campaign at home against Motherwell.

Celtic needed to win while hoping Rangers would lose at Rugby Park and although that never happened, the Hoops cruised to a 4-0 win. While the game couldn't truly be billed as a dress rehearsal for the following week's Scottish Cup final against the same side, the fans reacted to the loss of the league as only they could – with a mass impromptu Huddle.

That mass Huddle by the supporters was repeated the following weekend as Celtic ended the season by winning their 35th Scottish Cup when the Fir Park side were beaten 3-0 thanks to magnificent strikes from Ki Sung-Yueng and Charlie Mulgrew sandwiching an own goal from Stephen Craigan.

BIRTHDAY BHOYS
Beram Kayal - May 2, 1988
Davy Adams - May 14, 1883

FLASH BACK

25
May 1967

MOST of the 42 championships and 35 Scottish Cups won by Celtic have been claimed in May so it would be pretty hard to choose just one of them.

So, with that in mind, we've gone back to 1967 when both were added to the silverware roster at Celtic Park but, believe it or not, we are concentrating on another game for the month of May.

This was when all roads led to the Estadio Nacional and goals by Tommy Gemmell and Stevie Chalmers ensured that Celtic were the first British team to lift the European Cup as the Lisbon Lions beat Inter Milan 2-1.

CINEMA PARADISO

WHAT is your all-time favourite film? Have you ever wondered what your favourite Celts watch when they go to the movies?

Well, just before they broke up for the close season, we caught up with some of your heroes to find out what makes them head to the pictures and who are their favourite stars.

We also wanted to find out what turns them off when they visit the cinema.

So grab some popcorn and take your seat as the Hollywood Hoops settle down before the big feature starts...

GEORGIOS SAMARAS

Are you a regular cinema goer?
Yes. I will go once a week or every 10 days. If there are some good movies, though, I will go twice a week.

What is your snack of choice at the pictures?
Everything! Popcorn, of course, and maybe a milkshake – something nice and fresh.

Greatest film you have seen at the cinema?
The best ones I have seen are the *Lord of the Rings* films. But in terms of new generation at the cinema with 3D and high definition and everything, I think *Avatar*. I am not a great fan of 3D but I saw *Avatar* in 3D with my friends and it was a great movie. But my favourite films of all time would be the *Lord of the Rings* series.

Worst film you have seen at the cinema?
Brooklyn's Finest, I saw it before I went to the World Cup. Oh my God! It was a terrible film. I couldn't wait for it to finish!

Who is your favourite actor/actress?
My favourite actor is Denzel Washington. In all of his movies, he is unbelievable. I don't remember a bad movie from him. They are all top quality. My favourite actress is Sandra Bullock.

GLENN LOOVENS

Are you a regular cinema goer?
Yeah, I try to go once every two weeks, sometimes once a week.

What is your snack of choice at the pictures?
I am quite boring - just still water!

Greatest film you have seen at the cinema?
Recently, I have to say *Avatar*, just for the special effects and the impact it had.

Worst film you have seen at the cinema?
I have just seen *Hanna*, and I wasn't really impressed with it. It was okay but it was just one you would watch when you are bored at home.

Who is your favourite actor/actress?
I like Anthony Hopkins for his role as Hannibal in the *Silence of the Lambs*. I thought he was brilliant. I also like Jessica Alba, just because she is nice...

EMILIO IZAGUIRRE

Are you a regular cinema goer?
I don't really go here because they are in English and I don't understand them. I would go sometimes back home, but not a lot - maybe once a month.

What is your snack of choice at the pictures?
It's Popcorn.

Greatest film you have seen at the cinema?
For me it's *The Godfather*. It's a great movie and it was a good story.

Worst film you have seen at the cinema?
Pirates of the Caribbean.

Who is your favourite actor/actress?
I really like Nicholas Cage as an actor. He is always in action films and is very good.

To catch up on some more of your Celtic heroes visiting Cinema Paradiso, turn to pages 42/43.

PRE-MATCH PREP

YOUR pre-match routine probably means looking out your Celtic scarf and checking that everyone has their tickets for the big match before you leave the house.

But what about the men who are part of the Celtic squad you will be watching later on that matchday?

They each have their own way of killing time and preparing for the big kick-off - whether that's home or away, 3 o'clock on a Saturday, 12.30 on a Sunday or 7.45 in a midweek match.

Your Celtic Annual decided to find out just what the Hoops get up to in the hours and minutes leading up to the first blow of the referee's whistle.

MARK WILSON

Do you get nervous before games?
Yeah, I think it's only right you get nervous before a match.

How do you pass time on bus journeys to away games?
Probably just playing with my iPad or sometimes playing cards.

Do you have any specific pre-match routines or superstitions?
No superstitions really. And I don't think I do anything different from any of the other boys before a game really.

What is your favourite away ground?
I like going to Tannadice. I always seem to play quite well there when I've been back there with Celtic, and I have good results and good memories from there such as winning the league on the last day of the season.

Who has the oddest pre-match ritual?
Emilio is the only one I can think of. He always goes out of the dressing room last but then he seems to have to go out in a certain place in the line-up.

LUKASZ ZALUSKA

Do you get nervous before games?

Not really. I think when I was younger I was nervous. Now I am not nervous, I just have a little bit of expectation, which is like excitement. And I really enjoy every game.

How do you pass time on bus journeys to away games?

Usually, I listen to Polish music. And if it's a game being played quite far away, I might watch some movies.

Do you have any specific pre-match routines or superstitions?

There are a few. They are just small things really. I always put my right boot on first but this is not really something very strange.

What is your favourite away ground?

I think Hearts' stadium, Tynecastle, is really good to play at. The ground is really close to the pitch and it's always a good atmosphere. I always like playing there.

Who has the oddest pre-match ritual?

I don't know. But that is maybe because I just concentrate on myself before a game.

DANIEL MAJSTOROVIC

Do you get nervous before games?

Always a little bit - but in a good way. I think if you are not nervous then something is wrong.

How do you pass time on bus journeys to away games?

I play cards, speak on the phone or listen to my iPod. I just relax.

Do you have any specific pre-match routines or superstitions?

Not really, I follow my programme which I always follow before a game, and I don't have anything special I feel I need to do.

What is your favourite away ground?

Overall, I would say the Emirates as it was just amazing. That was with the Swedish national team against Brazil. First of all, the pitch was just amazing and the stadium was unbelievably nice.

Who has the oddest pre-match ritual?

I think Emilio. He always does his things all the time and is always the last guy out.

To find out how more of your heroes prepare themselves for the game, turn to pages 48/49.

SPOT THE DIFFERENCE

THERE are 10 differences between these pictures of Super Gary Hooper scoring against Rangers. The first one has been circled, but can you spot the rest?

Find out how you did by checking the answers on pages 62/63.

SEASON 2010/11 QUIZ

01   How many clean sheets did Celtic keep in the league campaign?

02   Which two Celts scored hat-tricks against Aberdeen in the same game?

03   Who scored Celtic's last goal in the final league game?

04   Which Celt scored on his debut at Hampden?

05   Who is the only member of the first-team backroom staff who didn't play for the club?

06   Which Celt joined the club for a second time last season?

07   Who was Celtic's top scorer in the Scottish Cup?

08   Which team did Celtic play first in the Scottish Cup?

09   Which three teams did Celtic play in all three domestic competitions last season?

10   After the New Year, which was the only month in which Celtic didn't play Rangers?

How did you do? Find out with the answers on pages 62/63.

JEEPERS KEEPERS!

WHEN Ronnie Simpson signed for Celtic in 1964 he was quickly nicknamed 'Faither' by his younger team-mates – after all, he had been playing first-team football since 1945 so he did have a few years on them!

And talk about being long in the tooth – Ronnie kept his false teeth wrapped up in his goalkeeper's cap in the back of the net during the European Cup final in 1967 so he would be ready for the photographs.

However, as soon as the final whistle went he had to run and rescue them in case they were grabbed as a souvenir by the supporters who immediately invaded the pitch.

MUSIC SCORE

ARE you in harmony with the Celts when it comes to music and who are the Bhoy bands that set their toes tapping?

In many ways the players and the supporters all sing from the same hymn sheet every time the Hoops emerge from the Celtic Park tunnel but the men in green and white all have their own tunes that they listen to before the match and in their spare time.

With footballers from all corners of the world now plying their trade at Celtic Park, the selection is wide and varied so you may see a new name or two cropping up among the stars you already know.

So get the headphones on and dance to the Celtic rhythm as during the summer we found out what the players listen to…

RICHIE TOWELL

What music do you listen to before a game?

I always listen to a CD that Charlie Mulgrew made for me. It's a bit of a dance CD that he used to play on his iPod before the games. It's really good. Even when I went to Hibs, I would try and put my iPod into the iPod station to play it.

Who is your favourite musical group?

Rod Stewart is my favourite and I know he is a big Celtic fan as well, so it would be nice to meet him one day. My Dad and my Mam always used to listen to him in the car. And as I was growing up I always just liked his music. Even now, I always have his CD on in the car or have it on my iPod.

What song would you like to be played after you scored a goal?

I really like the one they play now: *Just Can't Get Enough.* I think all the Celtic fans like it, too, as they are always dancing about to it, so I think that's a good one.

What was the last song you downloaded?

Beautiful People by Chris Brown. I like that song and I think he is a good artist as well.

What is your favourite Celtic song?

You'll Never Walk Alone. I think when that gets played before a Champions League game it makes the hair on the back of your neck stand up.

DOM CERVI

What music do you listen to before a game?

It's the Foo Fighters, actually. It's always kind of varied between some sort of rock and I think it was the Foo Fighters last year, too. In a weird way it's almost kind of superstition as it's the one playlist I don't shuffle. I put it on at a certain point and then try to time it from hotel to stadium and then I sit in the locker room for a little bit with my headphones to make sure I listen to all the songs.

Who is your favourite musical group?

That's probably the Zac Brown Band, which is country music – Oklahoma country boy, y'know. They are quite new. I have only known about them for a few years but I've liked them ever since I heard them.

What song would you like to be played after you scored a goal?

Obviously *Just Can't Get Enough* would be played at Celtic Park but if it had to be something else I'd say *Regulators* by Warren G.

What was the last song you downloaded?

It was *Sweat* by Snoop Dogg. I downloaded it last night.

What is your favourite Celtic song?

Just Can't Get Enough. I love it that it's catchy and the fact so many people are copying it. It makes you proud when people are doing something we started. I even heard it at an MLS game in Philadelphia at one point. In just a short time, it's become so huge.

For more sounds from your favourite Celts, turn to pages 58/59.

MAZE

CELTIC'S Emilio Izaguirre has to find his way from Glasgow to Honduras to take part in an international match and then all the way back to Celtic Park to play an important game with the Hoops. Can you help him get from Scotland to Central America and back?

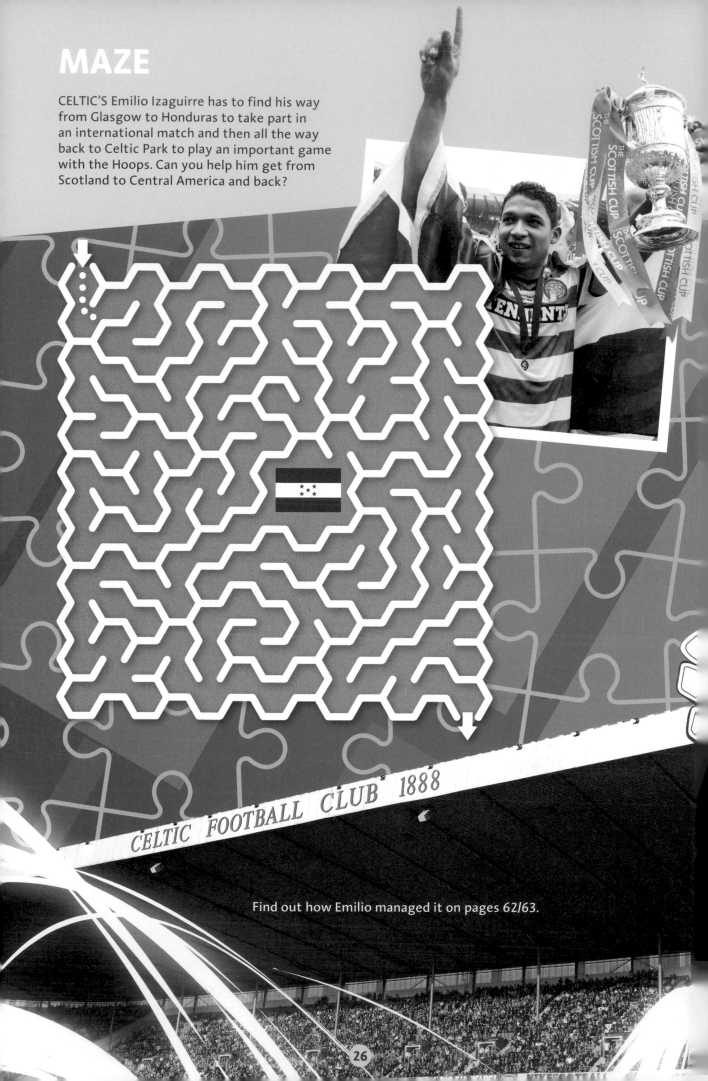

Find out how Emilio managed it on pages 62/63.

QUIZ QUESTIONS

01 How many consecutive League Cup finals did Celtic play in the 1960s and '70s?

02 In what year did Celtic first wear the Hoops?

03 Which season did Celtic play at Hampden?

04 In which two years did Celtic play in European Cup finals?

05 Who is the only man to have managed Celtic twice?

B	E	F	M	B	F	L	F	J	B	C	P	S
H	T	O	P	S	E	R	T	N	E	C	H	T
N	Y	X	S	Z	J	Q	A	T	R	O	P	H
F	I	Z	W	Y	R	T	F	E	N	F	R	G
N	F	P	B	P	I	E	P	D	K	C	A	I
U	O	R	S	O	A	O	U	T	H	F	R	L
R	H	F	N	Y	O	R	R	F	Z	M	S	D
J	E	A	W	H	A	H	A	A	W	C	S	O
I	L	F	Y	S	T	F	G	D	K	N	O	O
X	J	R	E	P	M	L	O	I	I	V	R	L
T	A	J	G	R	I	F	L	R	Q	S	C	F
G	O	V	I	B	E	A	K	Y	B	R	E	D
U	D	A	B	Y	V	E	I	U	G	S	F	E

WORDSEARCH

01 Country of birth for Emilio Izaguirre.

02 Hampden is the _____ Stadium.

03 Celtic's top scorer last season.

04 The Bhoys' heavenly home.

05 Is it a city game, or Kris Commons' former team?

06 They shine at midweek games.

07 Where the game kicks-off.

08 Top of the goal.

09 The man with the whistle.

Answers on pages 62/63.

JEEPERS KEEPERS!

ON October 26, 1963, Celtic were already 9-0 up against Airdrie when the Hoops were awarded a penalty meaning they could reach the magical double-figure of 10.

With the previous nine goals scored between the 17th and 64th minutes being shared by John Hughes and John Divers with a hat-trick each, while Charlie Gallagher, Bobby Murdoch and Stevie Chalmers hit a goal each, the crowd chanted for keeper Frank Haffey to take the spot-kick.

He thundered in a cannonball shot only to see opposite number Roddie McKenzie save the strike – Haffey duly applauded the save and the game finished 9-0.

CELTIC FOOTBALL CLUB

PASSPORT TO PARADISE

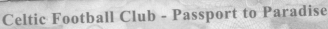

Celtic Football Club - Passport to Paradise

Passport

Position MIDFIELDER	**Squad No.** 67
Surname WANYAMA	**Given names** VICTOR
Nationality KENYAN	**Place of birth/Date of birth** NAIROBI/25 JUN 91
Signed 09 JUL 11	**Debut** V ST JOHNSTONE (H) 0-1, (SPL) 21/08/11

Previous clubs
BEERSCHOT AC, HELSINGBORG, AFC LEOPARDS, NAIROBI CITY STARS

```
MF<CELWANYAMA<<VICTOR<<<<<<<<<<<<<<<<<<
CEL67250691<<<<<<<<<<<<<<<<<<<<<<<<2011
```

Celtic Football Club - Passport to Paradise

Passport

Position DEFENDER	**Squad No.** 12
Surname WILSON	**Given names** MARK
Nationality SCOTTISH	**Place of birth/Date of birth** GLASGOW/05 JUN 84
Signed 16 JAN 06	**Debut** V DUNDEE UNITED (H) 3-3 (SPL) 28/01/06

Previous clubs
MIDDLESBROUGH

```
FB<CELWILSON<<MARK<<<<<<<<<<<<<<<<<<<<
CEL12050684<<<<<<<<<<<<<<<<<<<<<<<<2011
```

Celtic Football Club - Passport to Paradise

Passport

Position MIDFIELDER	**Squad No.** 8
Surname BROWN	**Given names** SCOTT
Nationality SCOTTISH	**Place of birth/Date of birth** HILL O'BEATH/25 JUN 85
Signed 29 MAY 07	**Debut** V KILMARNOCK (H) 0-0 (SPL) 05/08/07

Previous clubs
HIBERNIAN

```
MF<CELBROWN<<SCOTT<<<<<<<<<<<<<<<<<<<<
CEL08250685<<<<<<<<<<<<<<<<<<<<<<<<2011
```

Celtic Football Club - Passport to Paradise

Passport

Position	Squad No.
DEFENDER	48

ON LOAN

Surname
O'DEA

Given names
DARREN

Nationality
IRISH

Place of birth/Date of birth
DUBLIN/04 FEB 87

Signed
01 AUG 2005

Debut
**V ST MIRREN (H)
2-0 (SLC) 19/09/06**

Previous clubs
CELTIC YOUTH

```
DF<CELODEA<<DARREN<<<<<<<<<<<<<<<<<<<<<<
CEL48040287<<<<<<<<<<<<<<<<<<<<<<<<<2011
```

FEE PAID

HẾT GIÁ TRỊ SỬ DỤNG

Celtic Football Club - Passport to Paradise

Passport

Position	Squad No.
STRIKER	9

Surname
SAMARAS

Given names
GEORGIOS

Nationality
GREEK

Place of birth/Date of birth
HERAKLION/21 FEB 85

Signed
29 JAN 08

Debut
**V KILMARNOCK (A)
5-1 (SC) 02/02/08**

Previous clubs
MANCHESTER CITY, HEERENVEEN

```
CF<CELSAMARAS<<GEORGIOS<<<<<<<<<<<<<<<<<<<<<<<<<<
CEL09210285<<<<<<<<<<<<<<<<<<<<<<<<<<<2011
```

Celtic Football Club - Passport to Paradise

Passport

Position	Squad No.
GOALKEEPER	24

Surname
ZALUSKA

Given names
LUKASZ

Nationality
POLISH

Place of birth/Date of birth
WYSOKIE MAZOWIECKIE/16 JUN 82

Signed
01 JUN 09

Debut
**V FALKIRK (A)
4-0 (LC) 23/09/09**

Previous clubs
**DUNDEE UNITED, KORONA KIELCE, LEGIA WARSAW,
STOMIL OLSZTYN, ZRYW ZIELONA GORA, SPARTA
OBORNIKI, MSP SZAMOTULY, RUCH WYSOKIE MAZOWIECKIE**

```
GK<CELZALUSKA<<LUKASZ<<<<<<<<<<<<<<<<<<<
CEL24160682<<<<<<<<<<<<<<<<<<<<<<<<<2011
```

CELTIC FOOTBALL CLUB

PASSPORT TO PARADISE

Celtic Football Club - Passport to Paradise

Passport

Position	Squad No.
MIDFIELDER	13
Surname	Given names
MALONEY	SHAUN
Nationality	Place of birth / Date of birth
SCOTTISH	SARAWAK / 24 JAN 83
Signed	Debut
22 AUG 08	FIRST SPELL - V RANGERS (A)
	3-0 (SPL) 29/04/01
	SECOND SPELL - V FALKIRK (H)
	3-0 (SPL) 23/08/08

Previous clubs

ASTON VILLA, CELTIC, CELTIC YOUTH

```
ST<CELMALONEY<<SHAUN<<<<<<<<<<<<<<<<<<
CEL13240183<<<<<<<<<<<<<<<<<<<<<<<<<2011
```

Celtic Football Club - Passport to Paradise

Passport

Position	Squad No.
DEFENDER	22
Surname	Given names
LOOVENS	GLENN
Nationality	Place of birth / Date of birth
DUTCH	DOETINCHEM / 22 OCT 83
Signed	Debut
16 AUG 08	V FALKIRK (H)
	3-0 (SPL) 23/08/08

Previous clubs

CARDIFF CITY, DE GRAAFSCHAP (LOAN),
EXCELSIOR (LOAN), FEYENOORD

```
CB<CELLOOVENS<<GLENN<<<<<<<<<<<<<<<
CEL22221083<<<<<<<<<<<<<<<<<<<<<<<<2011
```

...all Club - Passport to Paradise

Passport

Position	
DEFENDER	38
Surname	Given names
THOMPSON	JOSH
Nationality	Place of birth / Date of birth
ENGLISH	BOLTON / 25 FEB 91
Signed	Debut
31 JUL 09	V FALKIRK (H)
	1-1 (SPL) 16/01/2010

Previous clubs

STOCKPORT COUNTY

```
CB<CELTHOMPSON<<JOSH<<<<<<<<<<<<<<<<<
CEL38250291<<<<<<<<<<<<<<<<<<<<<<<<<2011
```

30

Celtic Football Club - Passport to Paradise

Passport

Position	Squad No.
DEFENDER	17
Surname	Given names
HOOIVELD	JOS
Nationality	Place of birth/Date of birth
DUTCH	ZEIJEN/22 APR 83
Signed	Debut
11 JAN 10	V HAMILTON (A) 1-0 (SPL) 30/01/10

Previous clubs

AIK STOCKHOLM, HEERENVEEN,
KAPFENBERG, INTER TURKU

CB<CELHOOIVELD<<JOS<<<<<<<<<<<<<<<<<<<<
CEL17220483<<<<<<<<<<<<<<<<<<<<<<<<<2011

EMPLOYMENT PROHIBITED

18 JAN 2009

Celtic Football Club - Passport to Paradise

Passport

Position	Squad No.
MIDFIELDER	18
Surname	Given names
KI	SUNG-YUENG
Nationality	Place of birth/Date of birth
SOUTH KOREAN	GWANGJU/24 JAN 89
Signed	Debut
01 JAN 10	V FALKIRK (H) 1-1 (SPL) 16/01/10

Previous clubs

FC SEOUL

MF<CELKI<<SUNGYUENG<<<<<<<<<<<<<<<<<<<<<<<<<
CEL18240189<<<<<<<<<<<<<<<<<<<<<<<<<<<2011

HẾT GIÁ TRỊ
USED

USED

Celtic Football Club - Passpor...

Passport

Position	Squad No.
WINGER	49
Surname	Given names
FORREST	JAMES
Nationality	Place of birth/Date of birth
SCOTTISH	GLASGOW/07 JUL 91
Signed	Debut
30 AUG 09	V MOTHERWELL (H) 4-0 (SPL) 01/05/10

Previous clubs

CELTIC YOUTH

WG<CELFORREST<<JAMES<<<<<<<<<<<
CEL49070791<<<<<<<<<<<<<<<<2011

CELTIC FOOTBALL CLUB

PASSPORT TO PARADISE

Celtic Football Club - Passport to Paradise

Passport

Position	Squad No.
MIDFIELDER	14

ON LOAN

Surname	Given names
MCGINN	NIALL
Nationality	Place of birth/Date of birth
IRISH	DUNGANNON/20 JUL 87
Signed	Debut
01 JAN 09	V DUNDEE UNITED (H) 1-1 (SPL) 12/09/09

Previous clubs
DERRY CITY, DUNGANNON SWIFTS

CB<CELMCGINN<<NIALL<<<<<<<<<<<<<<<<<
CEL14200787<<<<<<<<<<<<<<<<<<<<<<2011

Celtic Football Club - Passport to Paradise

Passport

Position	Squad No.
MIDFIELDER	33
Surname	Given names
KAYAL	BERAM
Nationality	Place of birth/Date of birth
ISRAELI	JADEIDI/02 MAY 88
Signed	Debut
29 JUL 10	V FC UTRECHT (H) 2-0, (EL) 19/08/10

Previous clubs
MACCABI HAIFA

CB<CELKAYAL<<BERAM<<<<<<<<<<<<<<<<<<
CEL33020588<<<<<<<<<<<<<<<<<<<<<<2011

Celtic Football Club - Passport to Paradise

Passport

Position	Squad No.
MIDFIELDER	11
Surname	Given names
CHA	DU-RI
Nationality	Place of birth/Date of birth
SOUTH KOREAN	FRANKFURT/25 JUL 80
Signed	Debut
02 JUL 10	V SC BRAGA (A) 0-3, (UCL) 28/07/10

Previous clubs
FREIBURG, KOBLENZ, MAINZ, EINTRACHT FRANKFURT, EINTRACHT FRANKFURT (LOAN), ARMINIA BIELEFELD (LOAN), BAYER LEVERKUSEN

CB<CELCHA<<DU-RI<<<<<<<<<<<<<<<<<<<
CEL11250780

<<<<<<<2011

Celtic Football Club - Passport to Paradise

Passport

Position	Squad No.
DEFENDER	25

Surname
ROGNE

Given names
THOMAS

Nationality
NORWEGIAN

Place of birth / Date of birth
BÆRUM / 26 Sep 90

Signed
20 JAN 10

Debut
V HEARTS (H)
2-0 (SPL) 10/02/10

Previous clubs
FC STABAEK

```
CB<CELROGNE<<THOMAS<<<<<<<<<<<<<<<<<<
CEL25260990<<<<<<<<<<<<<<<<<<<<<<<<<<2011
```

Celtic Football Club - Passport to Paradise

Passport

Position	Squad No.
STRIKER	19

Surname
RASMUSSEN

Given names
MORTEN

Nationality
DANISH

Place of birth / Date of birth
COPENHAGEN / 31 JAN 85

Signed
01 JAN 10

Debut
V HIBERNIAN (H)
1-2 (SPL) 27/01/10

Previous clubs
FC BRONDBY, AGF

```
CF<CELRASMUSSEN<<MORTEN<<<<<<<<<<<<<<<<<<
CEL19310185<<<<<<<<<<<<<<<<<<<<<<<<<2011
```

Celtic Football Club - Passport to

Passport

Position	Squad No.
MIDFIELDER	20

Surname
MCCOURT

Given names
PADDY

Nationality
IRISH

Place of birth / Date of birth
DERRY / 16 DEC 83

Signed
19 JUN 08

Debut
V HIBERNIAN (H)
4-2 (SPL) 25/10/08

Previous clubs
ROCHDALE, SHAMROCK ROVERS,
DERRY CITY

```
WG<CELMCCOURT<<PADDY<<<<<<<<<<<<<
CEL20161283<<<<<<<<<<<<<<<<<<<<<<<2011
```

CELTIC FOOTBALL CLUB

PASSPORT TO PARADISE

Celtic Football Club - Passport to Paradise

Passport

Position	**Squad No.**
STRIKER	88
Surname	**Given names**
HOOPER	GARY
Nationality	**Place of birth / Date of birth**
ENGLISH	LOUGHTON / 26 JAN 88
Signed	**Debut**
27 JUL 10	V SC BRAGA (H) 2-1, (UCL) 04/08/10

Previous clubs
SCUNTHORPE UNITED, HEREFORD UNITED (LOAN), LEYTON ORIENT (LOAN), SOUTHEND UNITED, GRAYS ATHLETIC.

```
ST<CELHOOPER<<GARY<<<<<<<<<<<<<<<
CEL88260188<<<<<<<<<<<<<<<<<<<2011
```

Celtic Football Club - Passport to Paradise

Passport

Position	**Squad No.**
DEFENDER	5
Surname	**Given names**
MAJSTOROVIC	DANIEL
Nationality	**Place of birth / Date of birth**
SWEDISH	STOCKHOLM / 05 APR 77
Signed	**Debut**
16 AUG 10	V FC UTRECHT (H) 2-0, (EL) 19/08/10

Previous clubs
AEK ATHENS, BASEL, FC TWENTE, MALMO FF, VASTERAS, FORTUNA KOLN, IF BROMMAPOJKARNA

```
DF<CELMAJSTOROVIC<<DANIEL<<<<<<<<<
CEL05050477<<<<<<<<<<<<<<<<<<<<2011
```

Celtic Football Club - Passport to Paradise

Passport

Position	**Squad No.**
DEFENDER	3
Surname	**Given names**
IZAGUIRRE	EMILIO
Nationality	**Place of birth / Date of birth**
HONDURAN	TEGUCIGALPA / 10 MAY 86
Signed	**Debut**
18 AUG 10	V MOTHERWELL (A) 1-0, (SPL) 29/08/10

Previous clubs
MOTAGUA

```
DF<CELIZAGUIRRE<<EMILIO<<<<<<<<
CEL031005
```

```
<<<<<<<<<<<<<<<<<<<<<2011
```

Celtic Football Club - Passport to Paradise

Passport

Position DEFENDER	**Squad No.** 21
Surname MULGREW	**Given names** CHARLIE
Nationality SCOTTISH	**Place of birth / Date of birth** GLASGOW / 06 MAR 86
Signed 01 JUL 10	**Debut** V SC BRAGA (A) 0-3, (UCL) 28/07/10

Previous clubs
ABERDEEN, SOUTHEND (LOAN), WOLVES, DUNDEE UNITED (LOAN), CELTIC

DF<CELMULGREW<<CHARLIE<<<<<<<<<<<<<<<
CEL21060386<<<<<<<<<<<<<<<<<<<<<2011

Celtic Football Club - Passport to Paradise

Passport

Position MIDFIELDER	**Squad No.** 16
Surname LEDLEY	**Given names** JOE
Nationality WELSH	**Place of birth / Date of birth** CARDIFF / 21 JAN 87
Signed 12/07/10	**Debut** V SC BRAGA (A) 0-3, (UCL) 28/07/10

Previous clubs
CARDIFF CITY

MF<CELLEDLEY<<JOE<<<<<<<<<<<<<<<<<<<<
CEL16210187<<<<<<<<<<<<<<<<<<<<<2011

Celtic Football Club - Passport

Passport

Position STRIKER	**Squad No.** 27
Surname MURPHY	**Given names** DARYL
Nationality IRISH	**Place of birth / Date of birth** WATERFORD / 15 MAR 83
Signed 16 JUL 10	**Debut** V SC BRAGA (A) 0-3, (UCL) 28/07/10

Previous clubs
IPSWICH TOWN (LOAN), SHEFFIELD WEDNESDAY (LOAN), SUNDERLAND, WATERFORD

ST<CELMURPHY<<DARYL<<<<<<<<<<<<<<<<<<
CEL27150383<<<<<<<<<<<<<<<<<<<<<2011

CELTIC FOOTBALL CLUB

PASSPORT TO PARADISE

Celtic Football Club - Passport to Paradise

Passport

Position	**Squad No.**
GOALKEEPER	47
Surname	**Given names**
CERVI	DOMINIC
Nationality	**Place of birth / Date of birth**
AMERICAN	OKLAHOMA / 09 JUL 86
Signed	**Debut**
01 JUL 09	N/A

Previous clubs
MICHIGAN BUCKS

WG<CELCERVI<<DOMINIC<<<<<<<<<<<<<<<
CEL47090786<<<<<<<<<<<<<<<<<<<<<<2011

Celtic Football Club - Passport to Paradise

Passport

Position	**Squad No.**	
MIDFIELDER	4	**ON LOAN**
Surname	**Given names**	
JUAREZ	EFRAIN	
Nationality	**Place of birth / Date of birth**	
MEXICAN	MEXICO CITY / 22 FEB 88	
Signed	**Debut**	
26 JUL 10	V SC BRAGA (A) 0-3, (UCL) 28/07/10	

Previous clubs
PUMAS UNAM

DF<CELEFRAIN<JUAREZ<<<<<<<<<<<<<<<<
CEL04220288<<<<<<<<<<<<<<<<<<<<<<<<<2011

Celtic Football Club - Passport to Paradise

Passport

Position	**Squad No.**
MIDFIELDER	15
Surname	**Given names**
COMMONS	KRIS
Nationality	**Place of birth / Date of birth**
ENGLISH	NOTTINGHAM / 30 AUG 83
Signed	**Debut**
27 JAN 11	V ABERDEEN (H) 4-1, (CIS) 29/01/11

Previous clubs
DERBY COUNTY, NOTTINGHAM FOREST, STOKE CITY

MF<CELCOMMONS<<KRIS<<<<<<<<<<<<<<<
CEL15300883<<<<<<<<<<<<<<<<<<<<<<<2011

Celtic Football Club - Passport to Paradise

Passport

Position
STRIKER

Squad No.
10

Surname
STOKES

Given names
ANTHONY

Nationality
IRISH

Place of birth / Date of birth
DUBLIN/25 JUL 88

Signed
31 AUG 10

Debut
V HEARTS (H)
3-0, (SPL) 11/09/10

Previous clubs
HIBERNIAN, CRYSTAL PALACE
(LOAN), SHEFFIELD UNITED (LOAN),
SUNDERLAND, FALKIRK (LOAN), ARSENAL

ST<CELSTOKES<<ANTHONY<<<<<<<<<<<<<<<<<
CEL10250788<<<<<<<<<<<<<<<<<<<<<<<<<2011

Celtic Football Club - Passport to Paradise

Passport

Position
DEFENDER

Squad No.
2

Surname
MATTHEWS

Given names
ADAM

Nationality
WELSH

Place of birth / Date of birth
SWANSEA/13 JAN 92

Signed
01 JUL 11

Debut
V ABERDEEN (A)
1-0, (SPL) 07/08/11

Previous clubs
CARDIFF CITY

DF<CELMATTHEWS<<ADAM<<<<<<<<<<<<<<<<<<
CEL02130192<<<<<<<<<<<<<<<<<<<<<<<<<2011

Celtic Football Club - Passport t

Passport

Position
DEFENDER

Squad No.
6

Surname
WILSON

Given names
KELVIN

Nationality
ENGLISH

Place of birth / Date of birth
NOTTINGHAM/03 SEP 85

Signed
01 JUL 11

Debut
V HIBERNIAN (A)
2-0, (SPL) 24/07/11

Previous clubs
NOTTINGHAM FOREST, PRESTON NORTH
END, NOTTS COUNTY

DF<CELWILSON<<KELVIN<<<<<<<<<<<<<<<<<<
CEL06030985<<<<<<<<<<<<<<<<<<<<<<<<<2011

IT'S THE KOLKATA CUP!

CELTIC appeal around the world was further enhanced last year when the club played a major part in the prestigious Mahindra Youth Football Challenge in India.

The Under-14 tournament which aimed to improve the standard of grassroots football in the country featured teams from Bangalore, Delhi, Goa, Kerala, Kolkata and Mumbai, where 32 schools played the Intra-City leg to pick the champion schools from each particular city.

The six champion schools (Government Sports High School, Bangalore; CRPF School, Delhi; Infant Jesus High School, Goa; St. Joseph High School, Kerala; Sukantanagar Vidyha Niketan, Kolkata and Don Bosco High School, Mumbai) and their coaches underwent a four-day camp from April 21 to 24 conducted by coaches from Celtic.

The club donated 3,500 home shirts ensuring that all participants were kitted out in Celtic tops and this was a precursor to the Mahindra Youth Football Challenge Inter-City Championship, which was played from April 25 to 30.

In the end it was the team from Kolkata who lifted the trophy, beating Bangalore 3-1.

The final of the tournament was a thrilling encounter, with the favourites Kolkata taking the lead after just three minutes. But just a minute later, Bangalore equalised.

However, Kolkata scored two more goals in the first-half to take a 3-1 lead into the break.

There was no further scoring in the second-half and the boys from Sukantha Nagar Vidhya Niketan, Kolkata were celebrating their victory at the final whistle.

That wasn't all though, as based on their performance in the Inter-City Challenge, 22 players were picked for the final four-day camp in May, conducted by Celtic Under-19 coach Stevie Frail, Ian Coll, Head of Youth Academy Sports Science and Greig Robertson, Academy Coach.

Having watched the players carefully, judged their performances in match situations, assessed their physical conditioning as well as their technical acumen, the three most talented players from that batch of 22 travelled to Glasgow to train with Celtic for 10 days.

MAHINDRA'S TOP TRIO

THE three lucky young footballers from India selected to travel to Glasgow in August for a 10-day training programme with Celtic were Jayanto Mondal, Bishal Harijan (both Kolkatta) and Mani Maran (Bangalore).

Celtic Under-19 coach, Stevie Frail, said: *"The Mahindra Youth Football Challenge has been a great success. The Mahindra organisation, in partnership with Celtic Football Club, has put together an exciting project.*

"Celtic is very proud to be part of such a project. The enthusiasm and dedication of all the players, not just the selected 22, has been first-class and a credit to the boys, their schools and their families. Hopefully, they have learned something new and leave with lifelong memories."

Stevie Frail's Assessment of the Trio

Jayanto Mondal: Exciting wing-half with a good turn of speed and great control over the ball.

Bishal Harijan: Leading scorer in the tournament, this promising striker is worth his weight in gold and could develop into a quality striker.

Mani Maran: Hardworking midfielder with a good touch, great position sense and high levels of energy.

SCHOOL DAZE

YOU probably don't agree with the saying that "Schooldays are the best days of your life" at the moment – and you're probably not surprised that most of the Celtic players would probably agree with you.

However, we've transported a few of the Celts back to their school days to see how they got on and how they nurtured their football careers.

We find out what their favourite subjects were and what they could have been doing if they weren't playing football.

So eyes front, no talking and pay attention!

ADAM MATTHEWS

Do you have a favourite school trip?
Probably when we went skiing to Austria. I can't remember exactly where it was but it was a good laugh with all my mates. I was about 14. It was a good trip.

What was your favourite subject at school?
PE, as I was always good at sport and wasn't very good at anything else.

Did you play for your school team?
We had a very good high school team. We won the Welsh Cup and were UK five-a-side champions as well as being runners-up in Europe.

What job would you have done if you hadn't become a footballer?
I would probably have liked to have been a PE teacher and support and help kids achieve their dreams as well.

If you could give any advice to aspiring footballers, what would it be?
Just never give up, always believe in yourself. And if you get a rejection, just keep going and hopefully you will get a break.

KELVIN WILSON

What was your favourite subject at school?
PE for the obvious reasons, but I also liked drama.

Do you have a favourite school trip?
I was about 14 or 15 when we went to a farm in Derbyshire. It was for a week and we stayed in dorms. It was good fun and we got up to a few things there.

Did you play for your school team?
Yes, I played for my primary and secondary school teams. We weren't too bad either.

What job would you have done if you weren't a footballer?
I don't know, probably something in a trade, I'm not lawyer or doctor material.

If you could give advice to aspiring footballers, what would it be?
Be confident but don't think you've made it until you have made it. Keep your feet on the ground.

JOE LEDLEY

What was your favourite subject at school?
It was PE because of the opportunity to play football – and to get out of classes.

Do you have a favourite school trip?
We weren't allowed on school trips as we were that bad!

Did you play for your school team?
Yes, I was captain as well. We were okay and won a couple of trophies.

What job would you have done if you weren't a footballer?
A carpet fitter as my old man used to be one and had his own little business, so I would have done that, too.

If you could give advice to aspiring footballers, what would it be?
Always give your best and make that 100 per cent every time. And if you get the opportunity to play in the first-team, you've got to take it with both hands.

For more School Daze memories from the Celtic players, just turn to pages 60/61.

CINEMA PARADISO

IT'S time to spin the second reel of the big feature and find out what some more Celts like and dislike when they go to the cinema.

THOMAS ROGNE

Are you a regular cinema goer?
No, probably just three times in the last year - I always think I should go and see a movie but I never do.

What is your snack of choice at the pictures?
Well, obviously a bit of candy — wine gums or something and just water.

Greatest film you have seen at the cinema?
I'm going for *Blood Diamond*. I like Leonardo DiCaprio. He is a great actor and it's a good story as well. It's a good movie.

Worst film you have seen at the cinema?
I don't really know to be honest as I don't go that often so I usually pick good ones! I didn't like *No Country For Old Men*, though. It was meant to be a really good movie but I never got the ending.

Who is your favourite actor/actress?
My favourite actor would be Leonardo DiCaprio. He is always in good movies and when you see he is in a movie you know it's going to be good. My favourite actress would be someone like Angelina Jolie, Jessica Alba or Megan Fox - all the good looking ones!

JAMES FORREST

Are you a regular cinema goer?
No, probably just about once a month. I prefer watching a DVD.

What is your snack of choice at the pictures?
I always have toffee popcorn.

Greatest film you have seen at the cinema?
The Hangover - it was just really funny and I really enjoyed it. I prefer going to see comedy films.

Worst film you have seen at the cinema?
The Men Who Stare at Goats – it was out last year and it was the worst film I have ever seen in my life. It was going nowhere. Everything about it was bad.

Who is your favourite actor/actress?
Johnny Depp. He was really good in *Pirates of the Caribbean*. I've modelled my life on Jack Sparrow!

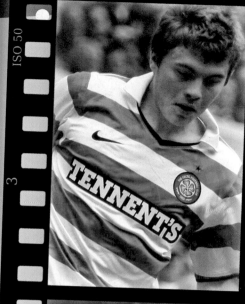

EFRAIN JUAREZ

Are you a regular cinema goer?
I go sometimes, but not regularly. Normally I go about once a month.

What is your snack of choice at the pictures?
I'll have popcorn and sometimes chocolate.

Greatest film you have seen at the cinema?
I would say *Gladiator*. The story about him is very good. It's inspiring, and he wins at the end. So it's very good.

Worst film you have seen at the cinema?
What is the worst? I just can't think of one!

Who is your favourite actor/actress?
Salma Hayek from Mexico. She is a very famous actress in Hollywood.

IZZY'S BEEN BUSY

FEW in Scottish football knew much about Emilio Izaguirre when he became Neil Lennon's ninth signing.

Despite representing Honduras at the World Cup and racking up over 40 appearances for his national team, spending his full career in his homeland for Montagua meant he was off the radar for many in this part of the world.

However, any qualms over his ability to settle into such a dramatically different environment and handle the rigours of Scottish football would be answered in resounding fashion.

When the prizes were handed out at the end of the campaign, the flying full-back swept the board, winning the SPFA Players' Player of the Year, the Clydesdale Bank SPL Player of the Year, the Football Writers' Player of the Year and Celtic's Player of the Year and Players' Player of the Year.

It was a remarkable achievement for someone who had only spent one season in Scotland but, such was the high level of his displays, he was a thoroughly deserving recipient of them all.

From his debut away at Motherwell, Celtic supporters knew they had a supremely talented player on their hands. He made an instant impression with his foraging runs down the left, wonderful skill and composure in defence.

It was a good start, but he simply got better and better, flourishing within Neil Lennon's expansive, attacking system, in which he became a potent weapon with his overlapping runs on the left.

That was ably demonstrated when he struck his first goal for the club in spectacular fashion against St Johnstone. After intercepting

possession outside the box, he casually flicked the ball over a defender, before slotting it under the keeper.

Time and time again, he proved to be the difference. He shone again as Celtic put Rangers to the sword in Paradise in March 2011 in an emphatic 3-0 victory. His bursting run down the wing and accurate cross into the box resulted in Gary Hooper netting Celtic's second goal of the game. Throughout the match, he was always an outlet for the Hoops, causing constant consternation to the Ibrox side.

And despite acquiring star-status following all of his accolades and exhilarating performances, Izaguirre is an unassuming and humble character off the pitch. A family man, his faith is central to his life, demonstrated by

his praying to the heavens gesture before every game.

Predictably, after such an impressive season with the Hoops, speculation mounted as to where his future would lie. But Izaguirre, grateful of the opportunity afforded to him at Celtic, has ambitions of remaining with the club and adding to his Scottish Cup winner's medal.

He said: "For me, I am very happy, with God, my family and Celtic. Since the day I first arrived here, the support of the people around me has helped me so much. I just want to stay here at Celtic and keep winning titles."

COLOUR ME IN!

CELTIC'S Israeli internationalist Beram Kayal is wearing the Hoops here and we want you to work your magic and bring this pic to life with your crayons, ink markers or paints.

GUESS WHO?

01

02

03

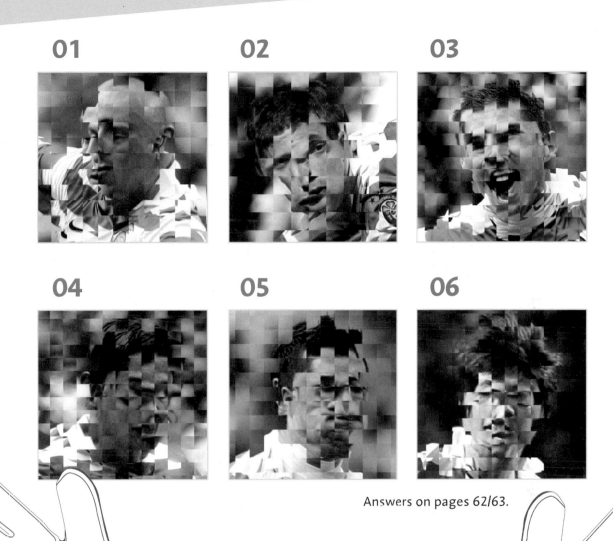

04

05

06

Answers on pages 62/63.

JEEPERS KEEPERS!

IN our previous *Jeepers Keepers* we talked about goalie Frank Haffey who took a penalty and missed but it didn't matter as Celtic were already 9-0 ahead against Airdrie.

However, in the Co-operative Insurance Cup semi-final of 2009 against Dundee United, the game went to penalties and, with both teams still deadlocked after the outfield players had taken theirs, the keepers were next in line.

Artur Boruc duly struck away the spot-kick past his future Celtic team-mate, Lukasz Zaluska, and helped the Hoops to an 11-10 win and the Bhoys went on to beat Rangers in the final.

PRE-MATCH PREP

IT'S time for the second part of our quest to find out how the individual Celts prepare for the game.

CHA DU-RI

Do you get nervous before games?

Yes, but this is normal. I think it's good for a player that he is a little bit nervous before a game, but not too much. But when it's kick-off and you touch the ball it's okay.

How do you pass time on bus journeys to away games?

Most of the time, I listen to music on my iPod or iPhone. And sometimes I sleep a bit.

Do you have any specific pre-match routines or superstitions?

Not really. But there is one little thing: When I go on the pitch, I try to go with my right foot first. I don't know why I started doing it. I think it was about four or five years ago I did it for the first time, and the match turned out to be a good game for me, so after that I have kept doing it.

What is your favourite away ground?

I haven't played at Ibrox yet so I don't know what it's like but I think Hearts have a good stadium. It's small but the atmosphere is very nice. In Germany there are a lot of great stadiums, particularly because they had the World Cup in 2006. So there are a lot of new stadiums but the best for me is the Allianz Arena in Munich. From the outside it looks like a UFO and on the inside it's amazing and is a great stadium.

Who has the oddest pre-match ritual?

I think 'Broony'. Normally, he is the captain and must go to the ref to choose which way we are shooting. But before that, he runs first on the pitch and makes a sprint three times and then comes back to the referee. He does that for every game!

GARY HOOPER

Do you get nervous before games?
No, I get more excited because I am going out in front of 60,000 fans, although there are maybe still some nerves.

How do you pass time on bus journeys to away games?
I sit next to Efrain. He doesn't speak much English so I just sit there and just chill and maybe listen to some music.

Do you have any specific pre-match routines or superstitions?
No, whatever comes to my head. I just take some drinks, get on with it and go out and play.

What is your favourite away ground?
Probably Ibrox as it's a big stadium with a good atmosphere and we have had good results there.

Who has the oddest pre-match ritual?
I have never noticed anyone really. I just get on with my own thing and concentrate on myself.

SCOTT BROWN

Do you get nervous before games?
No.

How do you pass time on bus journeys to away games?
Usually, I just sleep.

Do you have any specific pre-match routines or superstitions?
No.

What is your favourite away ground?
Cowdenbeath. I used to enjoy going there as a lad.

Who has the oddest pre-match ritual?
I can't think of anyone.

TREBLE TEENS

THE three trophies up for grabs at pro-youth level for the Under-19s and Under-17s all now sit proudly in the Celtic boardroom after the Young Hoops completed another magnificent campaign in Season 2010/11.

The previous term, the Under-17s narrowly missed out on the Glasgow Cup but came up trumps last season with a magnificent win over Rangers at Celtic Park while the Under-19s repeated their feat of 2009/10 by lifting the league and cup double for the second successive season.

The Under-19 Championship was the first to arrive when a comprehensive 4-0 victory over Motherwell on Saturday, April 23, tied up the title for the second consecutive campaign.

Just four days later, the Young Hoops made the short trip to Hampden in an attempt to maintain their superiority over their Ibrox counterparts in the Youth Cup final.

A fantastic strike from Greig Spence opened the scoring for the Hoops in the 71st minute but Celtic's domination wasn't enough to halt

Rangers from equalising just three minutes from time.

However, in extra-time, another wonder-strike, this time from Liam Gormley, tied up the game for the Celts and the Under-19s' Double was in the bag.

Then came the Glasgow Cup final for the Under-17s which the young Celts reached after playing in a round-robin league format against Rangers, Partick Thistle, Queen's Park and Clyde.

The smart money was on Celtic and Rangers making the final and that's what transpired and the majority of the 4,000 crowd at Celtic Park on May 9 were in raptures as the youngsters in green and white pinned back the opposition for the bulk of the game.

In the end, despite Celtic's pressure, there was only one goal in it but what a peach it was and it was a strike worthy of winning any final.

It arrived when Darnell Fisher won possession in his own half and found Paul George on the left side of the pitch.

The Irish youth internationalist then sped in on goal and unleashed a shot into the far corner in some style to lift the silverware for the Hoops.

Following the Under-19s' league and cup triumph, the Under-17s victory means the Celtic Academy are now in possession of every major trophy at pro-youth level in Scotland.

IN THE LION'S DEN

JOHN Clark has carried out nearly every job at Celtic. Most notably, he starred as the Lisbon Lions won the European Cup in 1967 and made 316 appearances for the Hoops.

After his playing career ended, he carried out various backroom roles in Paradise, including assistant manager and coach. However, for around the past 15 years, he has been employed as the club's kitman.

It's a job which has changed dramatically since the Lisbon Lion was a player.

Here, he gives us the lowdown on what is involved in clothing Celtic's players throughout the season.

How much has the kit-man's job changed since you were a player here in the 1960s?

Football back then was just making sure the kit was there. When I started here as a player you got a t-shirt and a sweater, and you didn't know whose sweater or shorts you would be getting – you just took it and it would be washed once a week! Now you might have to do a washing twice a day. It's a massive change regarding the working side of it. But the biggest change is the quantity and demands of everyone now. It's a huge business. Over the years it has got more professional. It's a really demanding job. You have to be organised and think ahead as you are on the go all the time. It's seven days a week. There is no break because of the games we have now - Saturday, Sunday, midweek fixtures, and you might have a reserve game midweek, too.

How far does your responsibility stretch throughout the club?

I deal with all the first-team players and staff, which is not just the manager and assistant manager now as you had years ago – it's an army! You could have 12 people along with the team. And you are not just talking the whole first-team squad. It's the whole full-time outfit at the club which goes down to the Under-19s.

How many different sets of kit do the players use?

Most of the players have three sets of kit and that does them for the whole year. They might have a double training session at Lennoxtown, and then you need to have one at Celtic Park when the team trains here before a game. In Europe, you have to have another kit to go away with.

What would you do first thing in the morning on a normal day?

You get yourself ready. There might be kit in the laundry from the night before. So you make sure it's put together, put in the lockers and ready for everyone coming. You are always in about an hour or more before they come in. So we make sure we are ahead of everyone.

Who looks after the boots?

The players are quite good at it. They all have an area where they put their own boots in. And when it comes the day of a game, Joe Hayes or myself will ask what boots they want and they go in the hamper.

What happens after training?

Myself and Joe make sure we get everything out for Angie Thomson to get washed and we help her out, too. We always share the

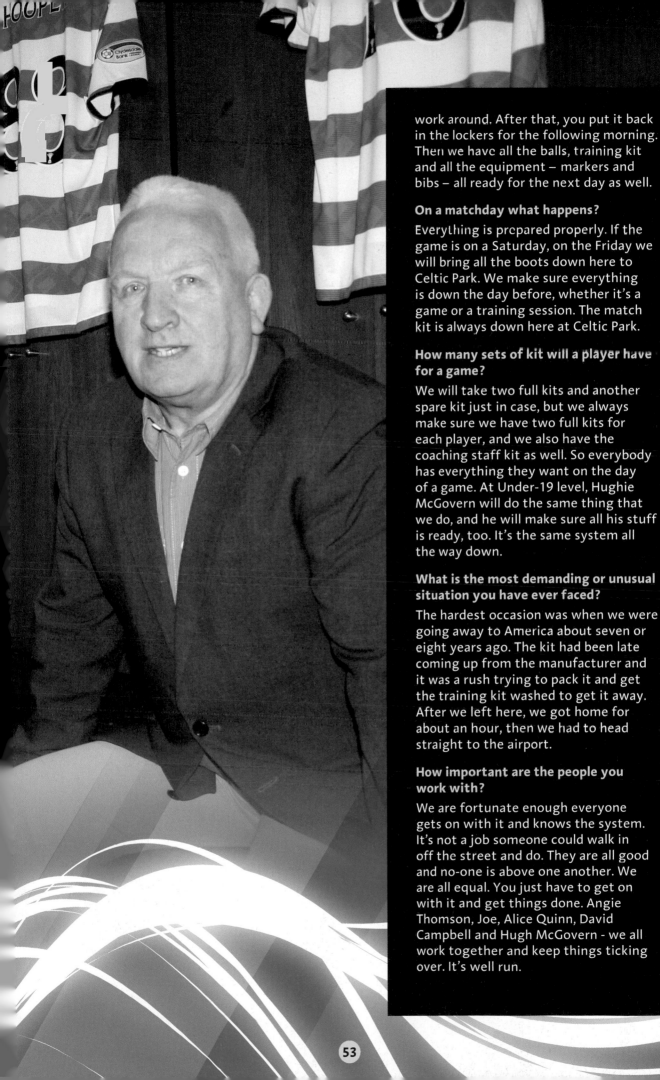

work around. After that, you put it back in the lockers for the following morning. Then we have all the balls, training kit and all the equipment – markers and bibs – all ready for the next day as well.

On a matchday what happens?

Everything is prepared properly. If the game is on a Saturday, on the Friday we will bring all the boots down here to Celtic Park. We make sure everything is down the day before, whether it's a game or a training session. The match kit is always down here at Celtic Park.

How many sets of kit will a player have for a game?

We will take two full kits and another spare kit just in case, but we always make sure we have two full kits for each player, and we also have the coaching staff kit as well. So everybody has everything they want on the day of a game. At Under-19 level, Hughie McGovern will do the same thing that we do, and he will make sure all his stuff is ready, too. It's the same system all the way down.

What is the most demanding or unusual situation you have ever faced?

The hardest occasion was when we were going away to America about seven or eight years ago. The kit had been late coming up from the manufacturer and it was a rush trying to pack it and get the training kit washed to get it away. After we left here, we got home for about an hour, then we had to head straight to the airport.

How important are the people you work with?

We are fortunate enough everyone gets on with it and knows the system. It's not a job someone could walk in off the street and do. They are all good and no-one is above one another. We are all equal. You just have to get on with it and get things done. Angie Thomson, Joe, Alice Quinn, David Campbell and Hugh McGovern - we all work together and keep things ticking over. It's well run.

DOT-TO-DOT

Join up all of the dots in this picture and see if you can identify the Celt in action here. Find out who the mystery Celt is on pages 62/63.

✱ Start Point

CAPITAL CELTS

Here's a list of some Celts and a list of capitals from around the world – can you match the player to his capital city?

Scott Brown

Dominic Cervi

Emilio Izaguirre

Efrain Juarez

Beram Kayal

Ki Sung-Yueng

Joe Ledley

Glenn Loovens

Daniel Majstorovic

Thomas Rogne

Georgios Samaras

Anthony Stokes

Lukasz Zaluska

Gary Hooper

Athens

Oslo

Warsaw

Dublin

Stockholm

London

Edinburgh

Washington

Tegucigalpa

Seoul

Cardiff

Jerusalem

Mexico City

Amsterdam

The correct answers are on pages 62/63.

JEEPERS KEEPERS!

A GOOD regular team line-up is every manager's dream and a strong keeper is essential to that team plan – but did you know that Celtic once played four successive matches with four DIFFERENT goalies?

To be fair, the games were in different seasons and, therefore, about three months apart but injury to Pat Bonner was a key element of this weird fact.

The Irish keeper played in the last league game on May 7, 1988 but had to drop out a week later and fellow-Irishman, Allen McKnight played in the Hoops' Scottish Cup final victory over Dundee United.

For the first game of the following season on August 13, Ian Andrews was between the sticks for the visit of Hearts in the league and just four days later, short-term signing, Alan Rough, kept goal against Ayr United in the League Cup.

SCOTTISH CUP FINAL
HAMPDEN PARK, GLASGOW, SATURDAY, MAY 21, 2011

CELTIC 3-0 MOTHERWELL

(Ki 32, Craigan og 76, Mulgrew 87)

SCOTTISH CUP WINNERS

AS the song says: "When the Celts go up to lift the Scottish Cup, we'll be there, we'll be there…" and those massed in the Hoops ranks at the East End of Hampden certainly let the world know they were there.

Over the years, Hampden has become almost a second home for Celtic and their supporters but, amazingly, each and every one of the Celts

TEAM

Forster; Wilson, Majstorovic, Loovens, Izaguirre, Commons (Forrest 82), Brown, Ki, Mulgrew, Samaras (Stokes 68), Hooper (McCourt 88). Subs not used: Zaluska, Cha.

who took the short walk up the stairs to collect their medal was doing so for the very first time as a Scottish Cup winner.

Manager Neil Lennon had lifted world football's oldest trophy on four occasions – the last of those as captain when the Celts previously lifted the Scottish Cup in 2007 when the Hoops completed the Double – and last season he

THE ROAD TO HAMPDEN

Fourth Round	Fifth Round
January 9, Sheilfield Park	February 6, Ibrox
Berwick Rangers 0-2 Celtic	Rangers 2-2 Celtic
(Majstorovic, Brown)	(Commons, Brown)

crafted a team that truly brought the thunder back to Celtic Park.

And this was his first trophy as manager as well as being Scott Brown's first Scottish Cup as Celtic captain to add to a day of firsts for the club.

It was also a record 35th win for the Hoops and the fourth time they have done battle with Motherwell at that stage in the competition.

The first was in season 1930/31 when Celtic won 4-2 after a 2-2 draw while the Hoops recorded a 1-0 win over the Fir Park side just two years later.

The most recent final between the two sides was 50 years earlier in 1951 when another 1-0 win was enough for the Celts.

However, with Celtic already being pipped at the post in both the league and the League Cup, they would need to show some resolve to ensure that it didn't happen for a third time.

It was South Korean midfielder, Ki Sung-Yueng who got the ball rolling with a wonderful opening goal when he spectacularly shot home from 30 yards as three quarters of Hampden erupted.

It was deep into the second half when the Hoops doubled their lead as a Mark Wilson shot was intercepted by Motherwell's Stephen Craigan who only succeeded in turning the ball into his own net.

And just three minutes from time, Charlie Mulgrew was contending with Ki for goal of the final when he thundered in a free-kick from the edge of the box...

And the party commenced...

Fifth Round Replay
March 2, Celtic Park
Celtic 1-0 Rangers
(Wilson)

Quarter-Final
March 16, Caledonian Stadium
Inverness CT 1-2 Celtic
(Ledley 2)

Semi-Final
April 17, Hampden Park
Celtic 4-0 Aberdeen
(Mulgrew, Ledley, Commons pen, Maloney)

MUSIC SCORE

AFTER that wee non-musical interlude, we return to the Celtic sound-system to find out what other tunes are reverberating from the Hoops dressing room.

KRIS COMMONS

What music do you listen to before a game?

The Kings of Leon. They are a decent rock 'n' roll band with good, uplifting songs.

Who is your favourite musical group?

That would have to be The Killers. I saw them live at Nottingham Arena and they were a different class. They have songs you can all sing along to and they get you in the mood.

What song would you like to be played after you scored a goal?

I think *Just Can't Get Enough*. When all the fans are singing it, it's class.

What was the last song you downloaded?

Give Me Everything by Pitbull featuring Ne-Yo Afrojack & Nayer. I just downloaded it the other night.

What is your favourite Celtic song?

It has to be *Just Can't Get Enough*.

PADDY McCOURT

What music do you listen to before a game?
Dance music. Charlie Mulgrew has a CD in there and we all just listen to that before the game.

Who is your favourite musical group?
U2 - just because I like their music.

What song would like to be played after you scored a goal?
I like the one we play just now, *Just Can't Get Enough*. It gets the fans going.

What was the last song you downloaded?
I have never ever downloaded anything or bought any kind of music.

What is your favourite Celtic song?
At the minute, *Just Can't Get Enough*. I have been enjoying it and the fans seem to as well. And I can see a few clubs have started copying us.

KI SUNG-YUENG

What music do you listen to before a game?
I listen to Christian music on the bus to the game as it makes me calm and relaxed.

Who is your favourite musical group?
Maroon 5. They make good music and have nice songs. I think every song by them is very good.

What song would you like to be played after you scored a goal?
That's tough. *I Got A Feeling* by the Black Eyed Peas.

What was the last song you downloaded?
Korean music, a singer who is very popular in Korea – but people won't know him here.

What is your favourite Celtic song?
You'll Never Walk Alone, because it's impressive when you see all the fans singing it with their scarves in the air.

59

SCHOOL DAZE

That's playtime finished now and it's time to return to the class to find out what more of your Celtic heroes got up to at school.

MARK WILSON

What was your favourite subject at school?
PE obviously, but I loved history as well.

Do you have a favourite school trip?
We went to Blair Drummond Safari Park. Classic! That was when I was in primary seven. I would be about 10 or 11.

Did you play for your school team?
I did – for St Ambrose High School and St Francis Primary School. St Francis won most things but St Ambrose were shocking.

What job would you have done if you weren't a footballer?
Primary School teacher, because I wouldn't want to be a High School teacher – that would be too much trouble!

If you could give advice to aspiring footballers, what would it be?
Work hard and always believe in your ability. And don't think it's going to be easy as most people think it will be. It won't be. Prepare for hard work if you are going to be a footballer.

CHARLIE MULGREW

What was your favourite subject at school?
PE. Anything was better than sitting in a class.

Do you have a favourite school trip?
We went to the Showcase Cinema and went bowling. That was the only school trip we went on!

Did you play for your school team?
We had a seven-a-side school team but I didn't play because I was signed with Celtic. I used to try and sneak and play but if Celtic caught me, I would get in trouble.

What job would you have done if you weren't a footballer?
A doctor or lawyer or something as I was dead good at school!

If you could give advice to aspiring footballers, what would it be?
Believe in your ability, work hard and be determined.

ANTHONY STOKES

What was your favourite subject at school?
I didn't have many, probably PE. Just because I could get out of the class and run about.

Do you have a favourite school trip?
The only trip I remember taking was going to Cardiff with the school for a few days. We went to see a rugby game over there. I think Ireland were playing Wales.

Did you play for your school team?
We didn't have a team, we just had little leagues within the school. But I played for the school rugby team for a few years, and I actually enjoyed that.

What job would you have done if you weren't a footballer?
I've no idea!

If you could give advice to aspiring footballers, what would it be?
Just work as hard as you can at your game and just be as good as you possibly can.

ANSWERS

SPOT THE DIFFERENCE (Page 22)

SEASON 2010/11 QUIZ ANSWERS (Page 23)

01	There were 23 SPL clean sheets for Celtic.
02	Gary Hooper and Anthony Stokes.
03	Paddy McCourt.
04	Kris Commons.
05	Garry Parker.
06	Charlie Mulgrew.
07	Joe Ledley with three goals.
08	Berwick Rangers.
09	Aberdeen, Rangers and Inverness Caley Thistle.
10	May.

WORDSEARCH ANSWERS (Page 27)

01	Honduras
02	National
03	GaryHooper
04	Paradise
05	Derby
06	Floodlights
07	CentreSpot
08	Crossbar
09	Referee